CW00661216

For Corran and Brodie
Twa o' the finest loons that I ken

First published in the United Kingdom in 2018.

ISBN number 978-1-9993161-0-5

DIV YE KEN
ONY DORIC?

Do you know any Doric?

CONTENTS

SPEAKING DORIC
Spikkin Doric

ABOUT DORIC
Doric is a dialect spoken in North East Scotland, around Aberdeenshire, Angus, Banffshire, Buchan, Moray, Deeside and Donside.

Speakers can use localised words unique to their own village. Accents can vary from place to place. A Toonser (city dweller) sounds different to a Teuchter (someone from a rural area) and spellings can also differ when written down.

The word for Seagull could be a skurry in Aberdeen city, a pyool in Gamrie and a Gow in Buckie.

It's spoken widely within the fishing and farming communities of the region.

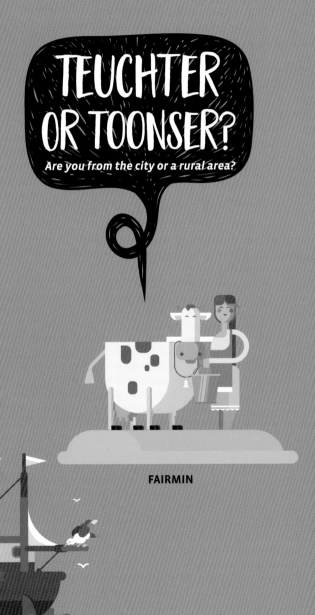

TEUCHTER OR TOONSER?
Are you from the city or a rural area?

FAIRMIN

FASHIN

1

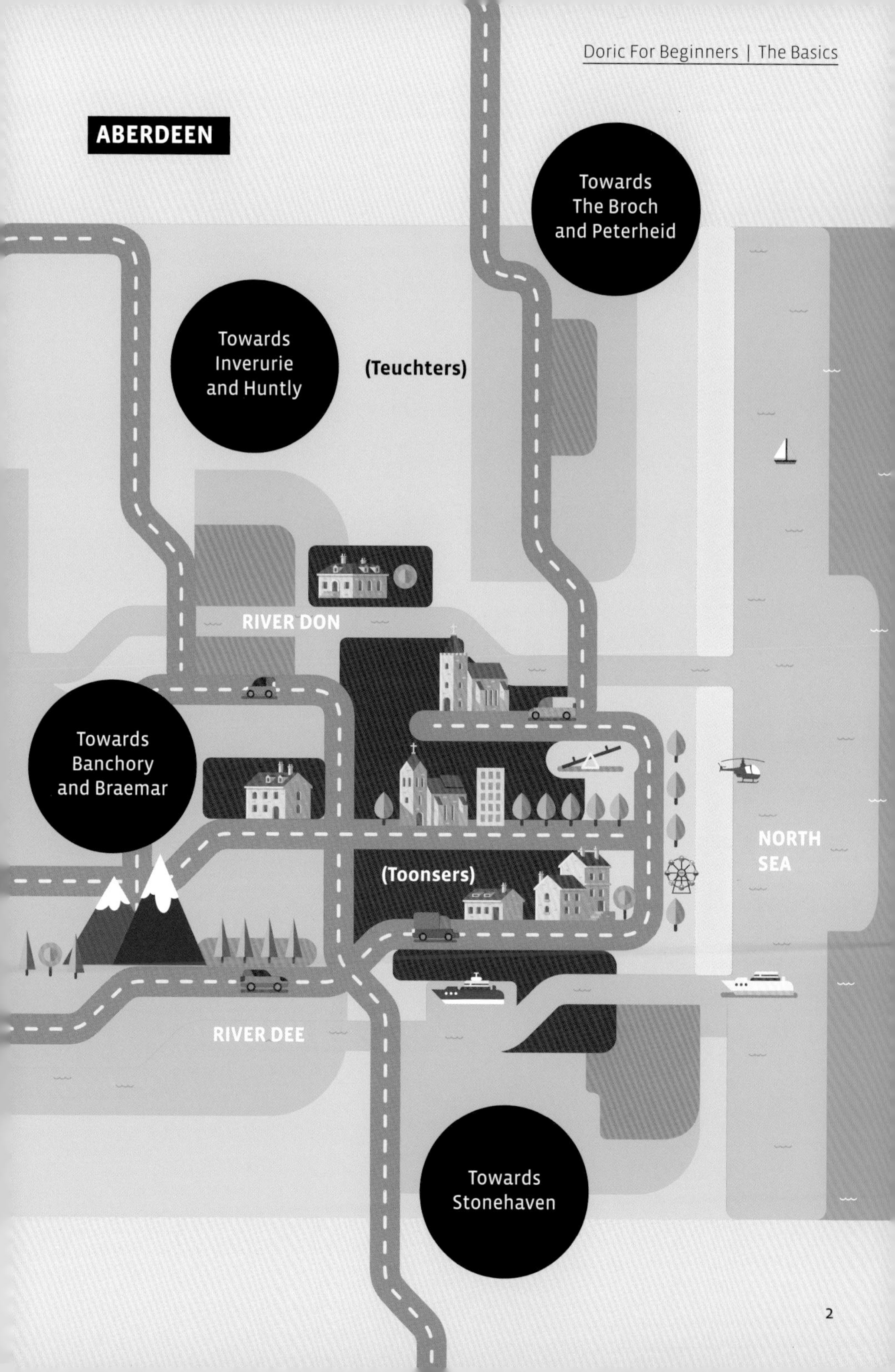

ABERDEEN

Towards
The Broch
and Peterheid

Towards
Inverurie
and Huntly

(Teuchters)

RIVER DON

Towards
Banchory
and Braemar

(Toonsers)

NORTH
SEA

RIVER DEE

Towards
Stonehaven

THE BASICS

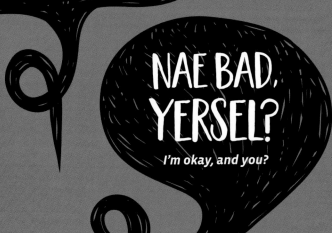

F WORDS

Some words with *Wh* sounds are replaced with a *F* sound instead.

FAR YE GAAN?
Where are you going?

FAN'S THE BUS?
When is the bus?

FIT'S 'AT?
What's that?

FOO'S YER DOOS?
How are you?

FA'S 'AT?
Who is that?

FIT WYE NAE?
Why not?

SAYING HELLO
Sayin fit like

AYE AYE MIN, FIT LIKE?
Hello, how are you?

FAIR TE MIDDLIN'
I'm not too bad

AYE, I'VE BEEN AWA
I've been away

I HINNA SEEN YE 'IS LANG FYLE
I haven't seen you in a long time

NAW, JIST CHAAVIN' AWA, YE KEN FIT LIKE
No just working hard, you know what it's like

I THOCHT YE HID GOTTEN LOST!
I thought you had got lost!

FOO'S YER DOOS?
How are you?

AYE, PECKIN'
I'm fine

BASIC WORDS

NAE No

NAE BITHIR
No bother

AYE Yes

I DA KEN
I don't know

NIT!
No way!

DINNA
Don't

DINNA DEE 'AT!
Don't do that!

I KEN
I know

DEE
Do

FINE
Nice

'AT'S AFFA FINE
That's very nice

GAADS!
Yuk!

CANNA
Can't

HINNA
Have not

I CANNA BELIEVE IT
I can't believe it

WINNA
Won't

**I HINNA SEEN
THE NEW MOVIE**
I've not seen the
new film

I WINNA BE GAAN
I won't be going

TELLING THE TIME

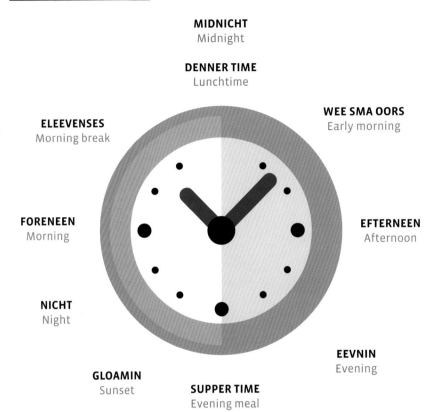

MIDNICHT
Midnight

DENNER TIME
Lunchtime

ELEEVENSES
Morning break

WEE SMA OORS
Early morning

FORENEEN
Morning

EFTERNEEN
Afternoon

NICHT
Night

EEVNIN
Evening

GLOAMIN
Sunset

SUPPER TIME
Evening meal

THE DAY Today	**THE MORN** Tomorrow	**YISTERDAY** Yesterday
THE NOO Now	**MORN'S MORN** Tomorrow morning	**EENCE A FORTNICHT** Once a fortnight
ES WIK This week	**MORN'S NICHT** Tomorrow night	**ONY TIME** Anytime
NEXT WIK Next week	**THE NICHT** Tonight	**SEE YE AIFTER** See you after
LAST WIK Last week	**THE NICHT AFORE LAST** The night before last	**SLATER** See you later

DAYS OF THE WEEK
Days o' the wik

MONDAY
CHUESDAY
WIDENSDAY
THURSDAY
FREYDAY
SETTERDAY
SUNDAY

FAN'S PEYDAY?
When will I get paid?

YE GAAN TE SEE THE DONS ES SETTERDAY?
Are you going to watch the football this Saturday?

COLOURS

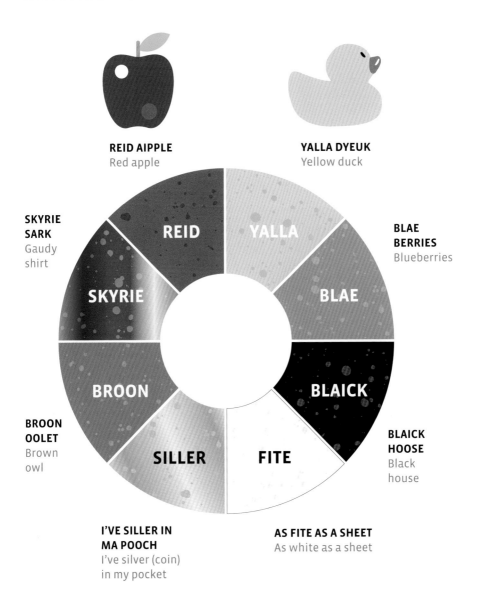

REID AIPPLE
Red apple

YALLA DYEUK
Yellow duck

SKYRIE SARK
Gaudy shirt

BLAE BERRIES
Blueberries

BROON OOLET
Brown owl

BLAICK HOOSE
Black house

I'VE SILLER IN MA POOCH
I've silver (coin) in my pocket

AS FITE AS A SHEET
As white as a sheet

NUMBERS

MONY A MICKLE MAAKS A MUCKLE
Many small amounts together
become large amounts

HUNNERS
Hundreds

THOOSANS
Thousands

NEEN
None

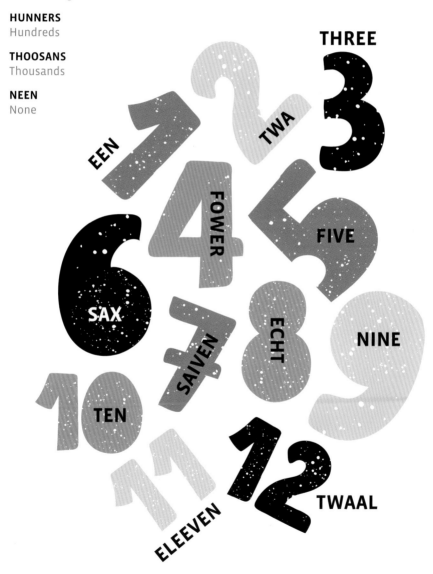

ACTIONS
Deein things

GING UP
Go up

GING DOON
Go down

TOUCH YIR TAES
Touch your toes

ON TAP
On top

GING THROWE
Go through

ANEETH
Underneath

ABLO
Below

GING INTO
Go into

GING OOT O'
Go out of

ATWEEN
Between

LOWP OWER
Jump over

AHEID
Ahead

AIFTER
After

AHIN
Behind

ABEEN
Above

ASIDE
Beside

TURN AROON
Turn around

DIRL AROOND
Spin around

PEOPLE

Folk

AUL MANNIE
Old man

AUL WIFIE
Old woman

MANNIE
Man

WIFIE
Woman

LOON
Boy

QUINE
Girl

BAIRN
Baby

CHIEL
Man

Faimly / Kin

GRANDA
Grandfather

MA
Mother

BRITHER
Brother

DA
Father

GRUNNY
Grandmother

DOTHER
Daughter

SESTER
Sister

KIZZEN
Cousin

FOOS THE WIFE AND GEATS?
How are your wife and kids keeping?

THE ELDERLY
Aul folks

AAL AGE DISNAE COME ITSEL
Old age doesn't come itsel

WE'RE NAE GETTIN ABOOT MUCKLE NOOADAYS
We're not getting out much

HE'S WEARIN ON
He's growing old

TEUCH AS AUL BEETS
Tough as old boots

I'M GYE SHOOGLIE
I'm a bit wobbly

CA CANNY, TAAK YER TIME
Be careful, take your time

A PEER CRAITER
A poor soul

CHILDREN
Bairns

KEEK A BOO
Peek a boo

HIPPENS
Nappies

KYKIN
Excreting

BUBBLIN
Crying

BABBITY
Baby

LITTILIN
Toddler

KITTLE
Ticklish

AT SCHOOL
At skweel

CLYPIN
Telling tales

SCUTTERIN
Time-wasting

DWAUMIN
Day dreaming

SWICKIN
Cheating

DINNA SKIVE SKWEEL
Don't cut school

**THE TAAK AA WILL
BE EFTER YE**
The School Inspector
will be after you

TIK AN TAAK
Game of tag

ILL-TRICKS
Mischief

PLEUKS
Spots

SMOORICHAN
Kissing

KINOODLE
Cuddle

YER CAT'S DEED
Your trousers
are at half mast

BEDDIES
Hopscotch

IN THE PLAYGRUN
In the playground

Een, twa, three a leerie
I spy Bella Peerie
Sittin on er bumaleerie
Ettin chocolate biscuits.

Eetle ottle black bottle,
Eetle ottle oot.
Fite fish, black troot,
Eetle ottle, you're oot.

Skinny Malinky Lang Legs,
Big banana feet,
Went to the pictures
and couldnae fyn a seat.
Fan the pictures started
Skinny Malinky farted,
Skinny Malinky Lang Legs,
Big banana feet.

Sticks and steens mey braak
my beens, but nicknames
winna hurt me.

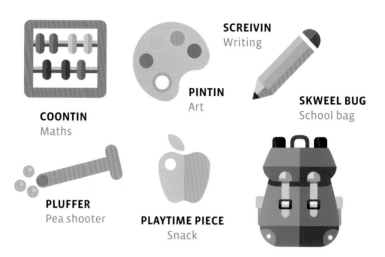

COONTIN
Maths

PINTIN
Art

SCREIVIN
Writing

SKWEEL BUG
School bag

PLUFFER
Pea shooter

PLAYTIME PIECE
Snack

HIV YE DEEN YER LESSONS?
Have you done your homework?

DIV YE KEN YER CARRITCHES?
Do you know your characters?

DOMINIE'S GAARIN THEM DEE SUMS
Teacher's got them doing sums

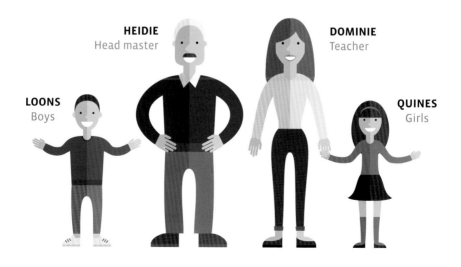

HEIDIE
Head master

DOMINIE
Teacher

LOONS
Boys

QUINES
Girls

DESCRIBING PEOPLE
Fit folk look like

STOATER
Fine fellow

LANG-SHANKIT
Tall person

SKINNY-MALINK
Thin person

SMAA-BOUKIT
Slight build

STRANG
Strong

STRAPPIN
Well-built

SWAAK
Agile

BANDY-LEGGIT
Bandy legs

LANG-NEBBIT
Long-nosed

GLEY-EED
Cross-eyed

UGSOME
Horrible

BAPPIT
Silly

BONNIE
Pretty

PIRN-TAED
Turned-in toes

SPLAY-FITTIT
Turned-out toes

DWEBBLE
Feeble

A CLIP
Pert woman

HUMPHY-BAAKIT
Hunch-backed

GYPE
Fool

GOWK
Fool

BONNIE HADDIE
Pretty girl

CLAIK
Gossip

SOOR-FACED
Sour-faced

EASY-OSY
Easy going

20

PERSONALITY TRAITS
Fit folk are like

BLATE
Shy

FEARTIE
Scared

THRIFTY
Frugal

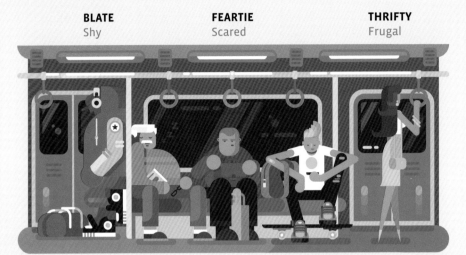

GRIPPY
Miserly

FINE CHIEL
Nice fellow

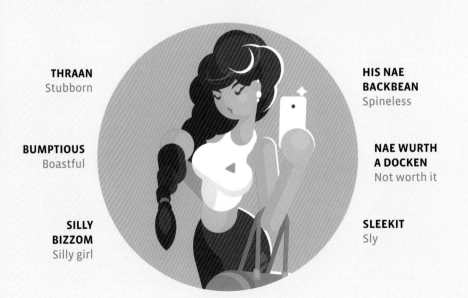

THRAAN
Stubborn

**HIS NAE
BACKBEAN**
Spineless

BUMPTIOUS
Boastful

**NAE WURTH
A DOCKEN**
Not worth it

**SILLY
BIZZOM**
Silly girl

SLEEKIT
Sly

ILL-TRICKET
Bad

THINKS HE'S AIRCHIE
He loves himself

WALLAGOOS
Buffoons

BIT O' A DWEEB
Bit nerdy

GOT GWEED BANTER
Witty retorts

GWEED-HERTIT
Kind-hearted

SOCIALISING
Haein folk in

SOMEONE'S KNAPPIN AT THE DOOR
Someone's knocking at the door

FREENS AN NEEBOURS
Friends and neighbours

COME AWA BEN THE HOOSE
Welcome, come through

DINNA BE A STRANGER
Don't be a stranger

I'LL HING UP YER JAICKETS
I'll take your coats

HASTE YE BAAK
Come again soon

TAAK THE WECHT AFF YER FEET
Have a seat

MAAK YERSEL AT HAME
Make yourself at home

YE'LL TAAK A CUPPIE?
Would you like a cup of tea?

THE KETTLE'S JUST BILED
The kettle's just boiled

WINT A SUPPIE MAIR TEY?
Would you like more tea?

WINT A FLY CUP AN A FUNCY PIECE?
Would you like a cup of tea and cake?

SO FIT'S AA THE CLAICK?
So tell me all the gossip

FOO MUCKLE SUGAR DIV YE TAAK?
How much sugar do you take?

HELP YERSEL NOO, THERE'S PLIN'Y
Please help yourself, there's plenty

JIST EEN SPEEN FER ME – I'M SWEET ENOUCH!
Just one spoonful – I'm sweet enough!

DATING
Romuncin / coortin

GIE'S A BOSIE
Give me a cuddle

HE'S FAIR TEEN WI THAT QUINE
He's really likes that girl

IS AAT YER LAD?
Is he your boyfriend?

I DINNA FUNCY ONY O' THEM
I don't find any of them attractive

HET LOVE SEEN QUEELS
Passion doesn't last

SHE'S THE AIPPLE O' HIS EE
She's the apple of his eye

HE'S GOT A HING-TEE
He's got a cling-on

THEY'VE SUPPIT THE KALE AFORE THE GRACE
They've been intimate before marriage

ARE YE TRAPPIN ONYONE IV NOW?
Are you seeing anyone at the moment?

THEY'VE MIXED THEIR MOGGANS
They've slept together

YE HUD ME AT FIT LIKE
You had me at hello

CHAT-UP LINES
Maakin a feel o' yersel

IS THERE AN AIRPORT NEARBY, OR IS AAT JIST MA HERT TAAKIN OFF?
Is there an airport nearby, or is that just my heart taking off?

DID YOU JUST GUFF? CAUSE YE JIST BLEW ME AWA
Did you break wind?
Because you just blew me away

ARE YOU A PARKIN TICKET? CAUSE YOU HIV FINE WRITTEN AA OVER YE
Are you a parkin ticket, because you have fine written all over you

DIV YE HAE A PLAISTER? I HURT MYSEL FAN A WINT HEELSTER-GOWDIE FOR YE
Do you have a plaster? I hurt myself when I fell for you

EXPRESS YOURSELF

SPIK UP NOO
Speak up now

FOO'S YER ERSE FUR CRACKIN PAN DROPS?
Are you in good health?

HERE'S A WEE THOCHTIE...
Here's a thought

FA'S YER BIDIE-IN NOO?
Who are you co-habiting with now?

YE NAE SPIKKIN?
Are you ignoring me?

IS AAT A FAC?
Is that right?

YE CANNA MAK A SILK PURSE OOT O' A SOO'S LUG
You can't improve upon something if it's unattractive to start with

AAT QUINE COULD SPEIR THE BREEKS AFF YE
She's very inquisitive

EXPRESSIONS

Lettin it aa oot

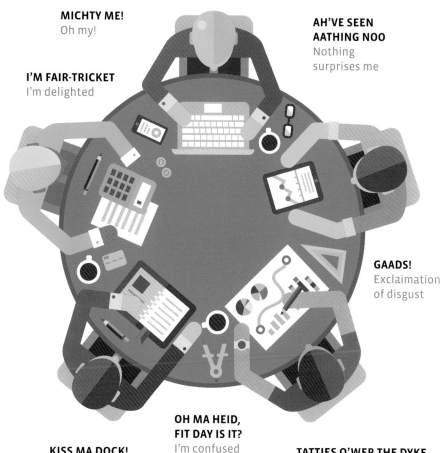

FIT A STOOSHIE ABOOT NAETHING
A fuss about nothing

MICHTY ME!
Oh my!

AH'VE SEEN AATHING NOO
Nothing surprises me

I'M FAIR-TRICKET
I'm delighted

GAADS!
Exclaimation of disgust

OH MA HEID, FIT DAY IS IT?
I'm confused

KISS MA DOCK!
Kiss my bottom!

TATTIES O'WER THE DYKE
It's all gone pear-shaped

EMOJIS
Foo yer feelin

FINE
Happy

GLAIKIT
Silly

HOBBLIN
Shaking with
laughter

FAIR TRICKET
Delighted

GREETIN
Crying

**BLACK
AFFRONTED**
Embarrassed

AILIN
Sick

BOKE
Puke

MICHY ME
Oh dear

IN AN ILL TEEN
In a bad mood

SMITTIN
In love

FEART
Scared

GWEED
Good

ILL TRICKET
Up to no good

**DOON IN
THE MOO**
Glum

FEEL
Foolish

TEXTING

FIT LIKE QUINE?

FA'S THIS?

IT'S DOD. MIND ME FAE LAST WIKEND?

OH AYE, DOD. AT WIS A GWEED BLETHER WE WERE HAEIN. FOO YE DEEIN ONYWYE?

AYE, NAE BAD. WIS WONDERIN IF YOU FUNCIED GAAN OOT ON SETTERDAY? WE COULD HAE A FLY CUPPY OR MEYBE EVEN A WEE SWALLIE?

AYE, OK. FIT TIME WERE YE THINKIN?

AT HOME

At hame

BROOKIE
Sooty

LUM
Chimney

REEF
Roof

HOOSE
House

WINNOCK
Window

PEENS O' GLESS
Panes of glass

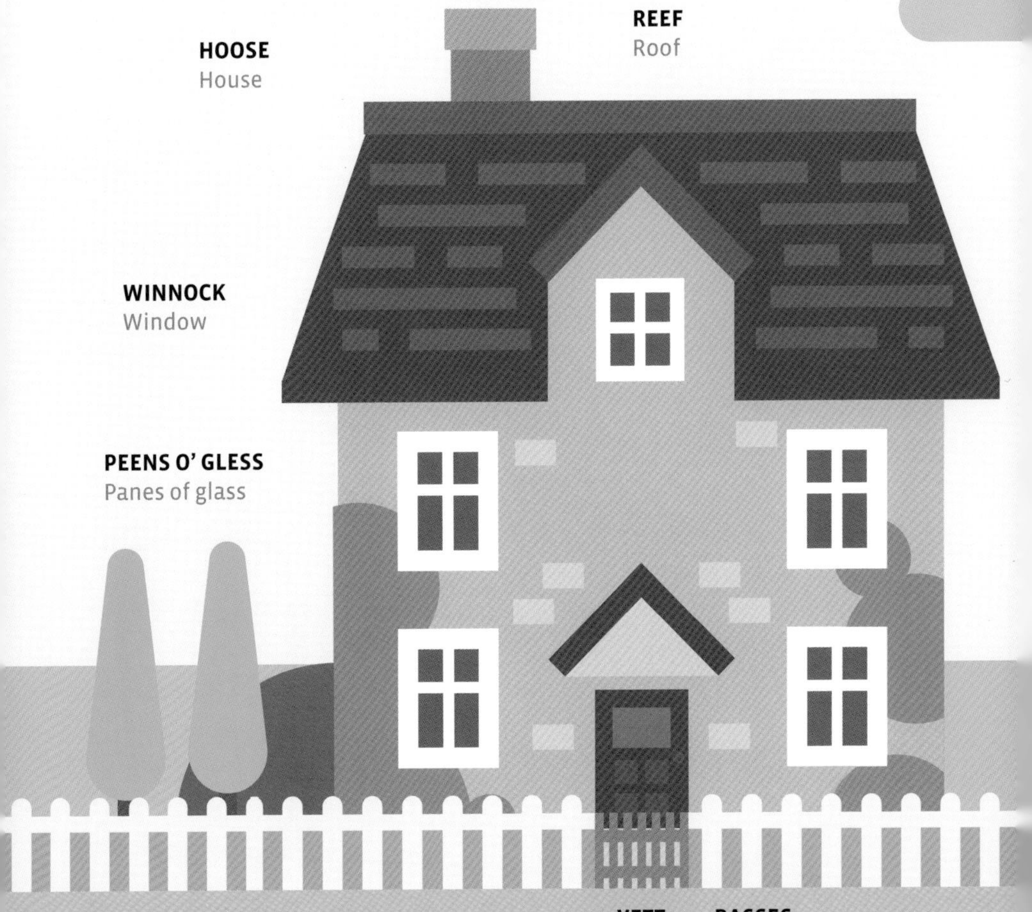

YETT
Gate

BASSES
Door mats

BAACKIE
Back garden

COOSHIE DOO
Pigeon

NEEBOURS
Neighbours

OOTHOOSE
Outhouse

AIPPLE TREE
Apple tree

PELLAN
Fence

THE LIVING ROOM

WAG AT THE WA
Hanging clock

KIST
Chest

FLOORS
Flowers

MUNTLEPIECE
Mantlepiece

CANNELSTICK
Candlestick

TIMMER	**LOWE**	**FIRIE**	**CAIRPET**	**BEUK**
Wood	Flame	Fire	Carpet	Book

SHE'S AFFA HOOSE-PROOD
She's house-proud

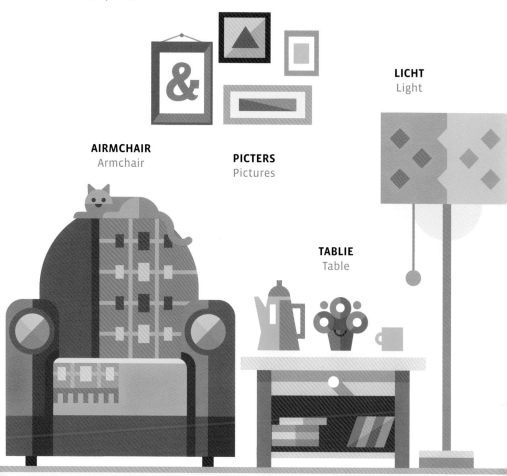

LICHT
Light

AIRMCHAIR
Armchair

PICTERS
Pictures

TABLIE
Table

SIT DOON AN TAK THE WECHT AFF YER FEET
Sit down and take the weight off your feet

COME AWA BEN THE HOOSE
Come on in

THE KITCHEN
The Kitchie

PRESS
Cupboard

BOOLIE
Bowl

SPEEN
Spoon

GIE THE POT A STEER WI A SPURTLE
Give the pot a stir with a cooking stick

BIRLER
Mixer

JAA HOLE
Plug hole

SPROOT AN PARE THE TATTIES
Peel and chop the potatoes

THE KETTLE'S ON THE BILE
The kettle is boiling

CLOOT
Cloth

AT KNIFE WIDNA CUT BUTTER ON A HET STEEN
That knife wouldn't cut butter on a hot stone

WAA
Wall

PIT AWA THE MESSAGES
Put away the shopping

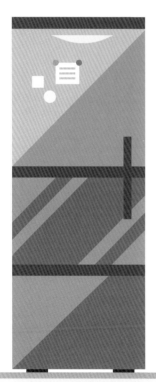

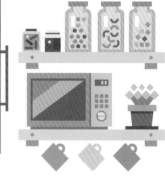

CUPS AN SAACERS
Cups and saucers

FLY CUP
Cup of tea

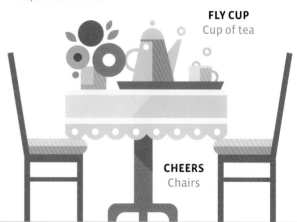

CHEERS
Chairs

**GIE THE KITCHIE FLEER
A SCRUB AN A DICHT**
Give the kitchen floor
a scrub and a wipe

KITCHIE TABLE
Kitchen table

THE BEDROOM

**STOP YIR FOOTERIN ABOOT
OR YI'LL BE BEDDIT**
Stop misbehaving or you'll be
banished to your bedroom

**FAIMILY
PHOTIES**
Family
photos

HOOSE PLUNTS
House plants

BEDDIE
Bed

PILLA
Pillow

STYOO	**SAFTIES**	**CHANTY**	**STEELIE**
Dust	Soft slippers	Chamber pot	Stool

THE BATHROOM

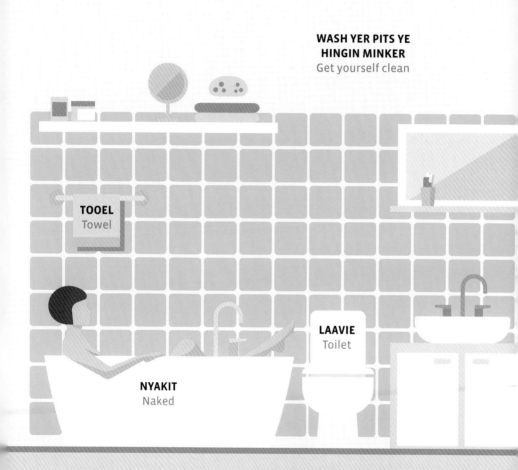

WASH YER PITS YE HINGIN MINKER
Get yourself clean

TOOEL
Towel

LAAVIE
Toilet

NYAKIT
Naked

SPIRK
Drop / splash

I'LL AWA AN COWP MA CAIRT
I must go and empty my bowels

WARDROBE
Claes

RIG OOT
Outfit

RIGGED OOT
Kitted out

GET YERSEL RIGGIT
Get yourself dressed

PIT ON
Put on

TAAK AFF
Take off

TOORIE
Hat / Bonnet

STRAA BUNNET
Straw hat

SARK
Shirt

FROCKIE
Dress

PEENY
Pinafore

BEETS
Boots

GYMMIES
Plymsols

PINTS
Laces

SHEEN
Shoes

MOCHLES
Fingerless mittens

GLAESSES
Glasses

TAP
Top

BRA
Bra

SEMMIT
Vest

SPAYVER
Trouser opening

POOCH
Pocket

PUNTS
Pants

DRAARS
Underpants

KYWTE / JAIKET
Coat / jacket

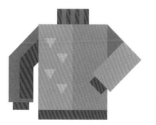

BREEKS
Trousers

SHORTS
Shorts

STOCKING SOLES
Socks

QUEETIKINS
Ankle socks

GANZIE
Jumper

PYOCK
Bag

WAAKIN BEETS
Hiking boots

THE GARDEN
The Gairden

BIRD HOOSE
Bird House

FOGGY BUMMER
Bumble bee

ROOSER
Watering can

FLOORS
Flowers

DUBBY BEETS
Muddy Boots

BLEWART
Bluebell

GROWTHE
Weeds

GARAGE
Garage

EX
Axe

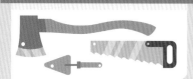

TROOWEL
Trowel

SAA
Saw

CLAA HAIMMER
Claw Hammer

TIN O' PINT
Tin of paint

CAARIE
Car

TIMMERIN ON
Working strenuously

FOOD + DRINK

AT'LL GAR YER INTIMMERS RUMMLE

That'll make you feel hungry

CHAT UP YER MAET

Eat up your food

AFFA FINE

That's very tasty

YER EE'S BIGGER NOR YER BELLY

You've been a bit greedy

A'M AFFA CLUNG

I'm very hungry

DINING OUT
Eatin oot

CAFE FEFTY TWA

OOTSIDE DINING
Dining Al Fresco

BLAIKBOARD
Blackboard

HIV YE GOT A TABLE FER TWA?
Can you accommodate a party of two?

I'LL HAE A MILK SHAAK
I'll have a milk shake

FIT CAN I GET YOOS?
What would you like
to order?

FIT YE HAEIN?
What are going
to order?

ROMUNTIC DENNER
Romantic meal

HUDDIN HAANS
Holding hands

BREAKFAST

BLAICK COFFEE
Filter coffee

BUTTERY / ROWIE
Savoury pastry

BIL'T EGG
Boiled egg

LORNE SAASAGE
Square sausage

TATTIE SCONE
Potato scone

I'LL HAE THE HALE JING BANG
Can I have a full Scottish breakfast please?

HAGGIS
Haggis

BLAICK PUDDIN
Black Pudding

SAASAGE
Sausage

PORRITCH AN TREYCLE
Porridge and treacle

BACON ROLL
Bacon in a bun

KIPPERS
Smoked herring

FITE BREID
White bread

JEELY CAN
Jam jar

FLOORY BAP / SOFTIE
Floury roll

BANNOCKS
Pancakes

SNACKS

A FLY CUP
Odd cup of tea

JEELIE PIECE
Jam sandwich

BROKENERS
Broken biscuits from
a Bakers sold cheaply

CAPPIE
Ice-cream cone

A FUNCY PIECE
A sweet treat like a
cake or a doughnut

FOOSTIE
Stale

BREID
Bread

POTTIT HEID
Potted head

**SOOR
PLOOMS**
Sour plums

**BASKETIE
O' FRUIT**
Fruit basket

SCOOF
Swig

SUP
Drink

GALSHIKS
Sweeties

ALE
Soft drink

LUNCH

GINGER BREID MANNIE
Ginger bread man

PRAWNIES
Prawns

CHUCKEN AN SKILRLIE
Chicken with oatmeal stuffing

BROSE
Oatmeal and boiled water

FINNAN HADDIE
Smoked Haddock from Findon

ARBROATH SMOKIE
Smoked fish from Arbroath

HERRIN
Herring

CUBBAGE
Cabbage

TATTIES
Potatoes

SPROOTS
Sprouts

HINGIN INGINS
Hanging onions

MEELIE / FYTE PUDDIN
White pudding made from oatmeal

A CAIRRY OOT
Take away

EVENING MEAL

A RECHT DENNER
a good meal

CULLEN SKINK
Smoked haddock soup

HOTCH-POTCH
Mutton broth

BURNS SUPPER
Haggis, neeps and tatties

TROOT
Trout

FINE PUDDIN
Desert

JEELIP
A ladleful

AN EGGIE FOR YOUR TEA
Egg

GLAESS O' REID
Red wine

STOVIES
Leftover meat, potatoes and onions

FISH SUPPER
Haddock and chips

SHOPPING
Messages

I'M AWA TE THE SHOPPIE TE DEE MA EERINS
I'm going to do my shopping

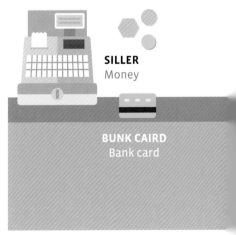

SILLER
Money

BUNK CAIRD
Bank card

QUANTITIES
Foo much

HILLOCK O'...
A great number of...

WEE SUPPY
A small bit / small sip

BOORACH O'...
A cluster of...

SKIFFIN
Light amount

JING BANG
Whole amount

A PUCKLE O'...
A small bit of...

A NIPPICK O'...
A small piece of...

KIBOODLE
Entire amount

A MUCKLE O'...
A large bit of

TEENY-WEENY
Tiny

SONSIE
Plump

A RICKLE O'...
A loose pile of...

A PUN O' HINGIN MINCE
A pound of sausages

A BILIN O' TATTIES
Enough potatoes for one meal

IN THE PUB

In the pub

FUSKY GLAESS
Whisky glass

DRAM
Drink

BIRLING
Drinking match

DROOTHY
Thirsty

DINNA DROON THE MILLER
Don't put too much water in my whisky

SNIFTER
Small dram

HE TAAKS A BUCKET
He can drink a vast amount

AWA WI IT

OOT THE GAME

STOCIOUS

PISHED

BOOZY

RAT-ARSED

BLEEZIN

BUCKLED

SH*T MIRACKED

BLOOTERED

SOTTERED

GUTTERED

RUBBERED

FAA'IN DOON

HOWLIN

SOZZLED

FU

HAMMERED

MINCED

MINKIT

SLOSHED

MORTAL

STEAMBOATS

STOTTIN

PANJOTERALISED

TOTALLY MINGIN

TOOTEROO

TUNKED-UP

STEAMIN

WHEELS HIV COME AFF

TATTIES OWER THE SIDE

THE OUTDOORS

The Ootdoors

HULLS
Hills

HEDDER
Heather

LYTHE
Shelter

CWYLE
Glowing ember

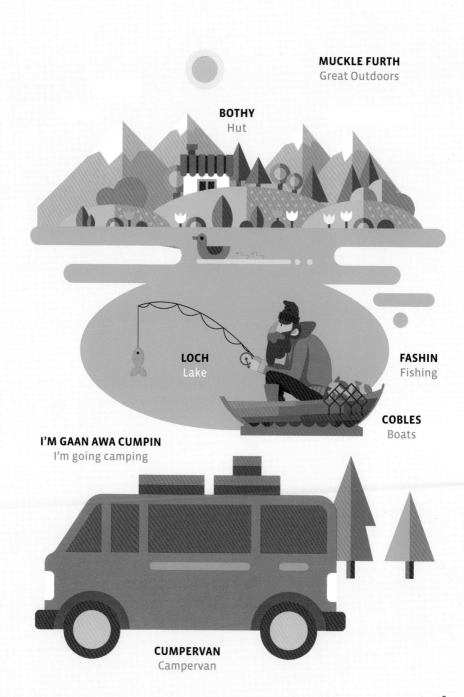

MUCKLE FURTH
Great Outdoors

BOTHY
Hut

LOCH
Lake

FASHIN
Fishing

COBLES
Boats

I'M GAAN AWA CUMPIN
I'm going camping

CUMPERVAN
Campervan

THE SEASONS

SPRING

SUMMER
Simmer

**NE'ER CAST A CLOUT
TILL MEY BE OOT**
Never throw away
warm clothes until
May has passed

THE NICHTS ARE CREEPIN OOT
Spring is on the way

**APRIL SHOOERS,
MEY FLOOERS**
April showers, May flowers

**THE EVENIN REED AND
MORNIN GREY IS AYE THE
SIGN O' A BONNY DAY**
Red sky at night and
a grey morning mean
it's going to be a nice day

FIT A BONNY GLOAMIN
What a nice sunset

AUTUMN
Backeyn

WINTER

**THE NICHTS ARE
FAIRLY DRAAWIN IN**
Autumn is on it's way

BOGLES
Ghosts

DOOKIN FOR AIPLES
Ducking for apples

TATTIE HOWKIN
Tattie picking

**FIN ROON THE MEEN THERE IS A BROCH
THE WITHER WILL BE CAAL AN ROCH**
When the moon has a halo,
the weather will be cold and rough

SNAAMEN
Snowmen

SUNTIE CLAAS
Santa Claus

CAAL LUGS
Cold ears

THE WEATHER
The Wither

I'M DROOKIT
I'm soaking wet

SAPPEN WEET
Soaking wet

PLOOTER
Rain

SMIRRY
Drizzling

IT'S DINGIN DOON
It's raining

POORIN O RAIN
Raining

PLOWT
Heavy shower

THREATNIN
Overcast

HOPE THE RAIN BIDES AFF FOR YOU
Hope it stays dry

IT'S GYE WAARM
It's very warm

WATERGAW
Rainbow

MOCHY
Muggy

PLOTTIN
Unusually hot

SNELL WIN
Cutting wind

WEET
Wet

IT'S BLAAIN A RICHT BLEESTER
It's very windy

IT'S SKYTIE
It's icey

IT'S SNAAIN
It's snowing

THE HAAR'S ROLLIN IN
The sea fog is coming in

SNAA BREE
Slush

OWER HET
Too hot

BILEIN HET
Boiling hot

DID YE SEE THE MERRY DANCERS LAST NICHT?
Did you see the Northern Lights last night?

HET
Hot

WAREM
Warm

THUNNER PLUMP
Thunder shower

NAE BAD
Mild

CAAL
Cold

FIT A DREICH DAY
It's a miserable day

BALTIC
Freezing

62

DOWN ON THE FARM
Doon on the fairm

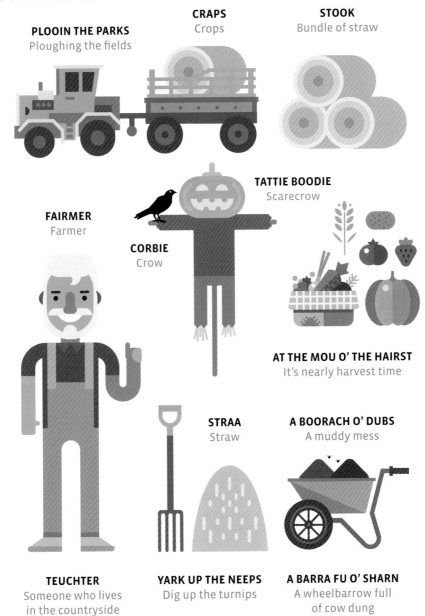

CRAPS
Crops

STOOK
Bundle of straw

PLOOIN THE PARKS
Ploughing the fields

FAIRMER
Farmer

CORBIE
Crow

TATTIE BOODIE
Scarecrow

AT THE MOU O' THE HAIRST
It's nearly harvest time

STRAA
Straw

A BOORACH O' DUBS
A muddy mess

TEUCHTER
Someone who lives
in the countryside

YARK UP THE NEEPS
Dig up the turnips

A BARRA FU O' SHARN
A wheelbarrow full
of cow dung

THE BEESE / NOWT
Cattle

STIRKIES
Bullocks

SHELT
Pony

MILKIN STEELIE
Milking stool

COO / KYE
Cow

FES THE KYE IN TE BE MILKIT
Fetch the cow for milking

SHARNY DUBS
Manure

TUP
Ram

YOWE
Sheep

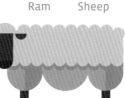

SOO
Sow

GET THE CLIPPIN DEEN
Shear the sheep

GRUMPHIE
Pig

GIMMER
Sheep with one lamb

HOGG
Young sheep

COCKALEERIE
Cockerel

CHUCKNEYS
Chickens

KNAPDARLOCHS
Matted dung on the hind quarters of cattle or sheep

FAIRM DUG
Farm dog

KITTLEN
Kitten

DYEUK
Duck

64

DOWN THE PARK
Doon the park

TAAK A PEW
Have a seat

HAEIN A SHOTTIE O' A BIKE
Cycling

LUBSTER REED
Sunburnt

GIRSE
Grass

FINE DAY
Nice weather

TEEN THE DUG OOT
Walking the dog

DYEUK POND
Duck pond

PUSH THE BAIRN
Push the child

COACH
Pram

DOWN THE BEACH

Doon the beach

BOULIE-BASHERS
Youths who frequent
the Beach Boulevard

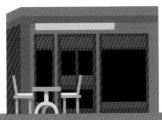

DELLIN
Digging

SKURRY / PYOOL / GOW
Seagull

DUNTER
Dolphin

SPREEF
Beachcomb

FLUKES
Flounders

SELKIE
Seal

SILLER DARLINS
Herring

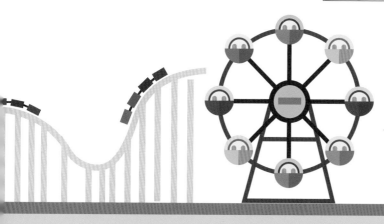

THE AIBERDEEN EE
Ferris wheel
at Codonas

**THE SILLER CITY WI
THE GOWD'N SANS**
The silver city with
the golden sands

BUCKIE
Periwinkle

CAPPIE
Ice-cream

PARTAN
Crab

DULSE
Seaweed

CLUNKERTONIE
Jellyfish

DOOKERS
Swimming
costume

ANIMALS

Critters

AT MANNIE IS A PEER CRAITER

That man's a poor creature

FOBBIN LIKE A FAT KITTLIN

Panting

CAAT
Cat

RUBBIT
Rabbit

DUG
Dog

TED
Toad

MOOSE
Mouse

MYAAKINS
Hares

PUDDOCK
Frog

A MUCKLE PUDDOCK
Toad

TOD
Fox

MOWDIEWORTS
Mole

SELKIE
Seal

FUTRET
Ferret

INSECTS
Beesties

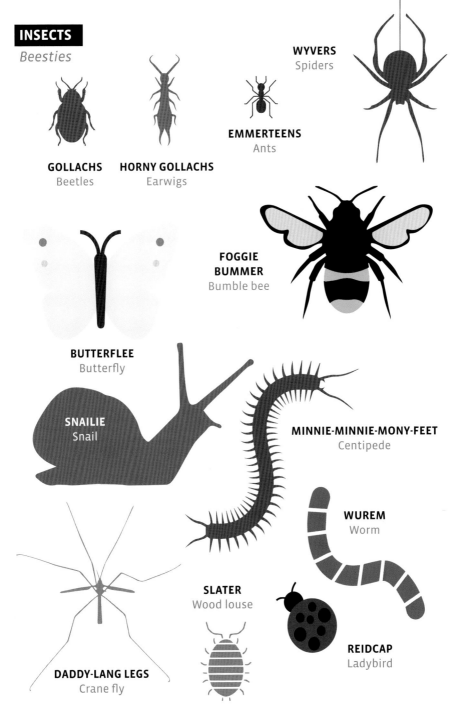

GOLLACHS
Beetles

HORNY GOLLACHS
Earwigs

EMMERTEENS
Ants

WYVERS
Spiders

FOGGIE BUMMER
Bumble bee

BUTTERFLEE
Butterfly

SNAILIE
Snail

MINNIE-MINNIE-MONY-FEET
Centipede

WUREM
Worm

DADDY-LANG LEGS
Crane fly

SLATER
Wood louse

REIDCAP
Ladybird

BIRDS

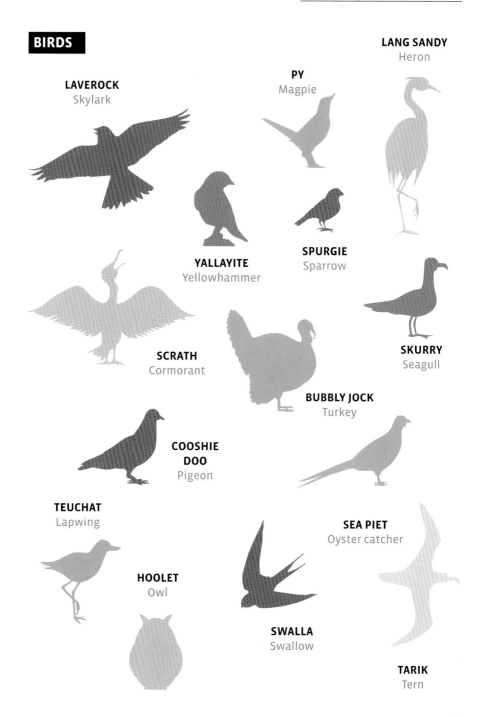

LANG SANDY
Heron

PY
Magpie

LAVEROCK
Skylark

YALLAYITE
Yellowhammer

SPURGIE
Sparrow

SCRATH
Cormorant

SKURRY
Seagull

BUBBLY JOCK
Turkey

COOSHIE DOO
Pigeon

TEUCHAT
Lapwing

SEA PIET
Oyster catcher

HOOLET
Owl

SWALLA
Swallow

TARIK
Tern

HEALTH

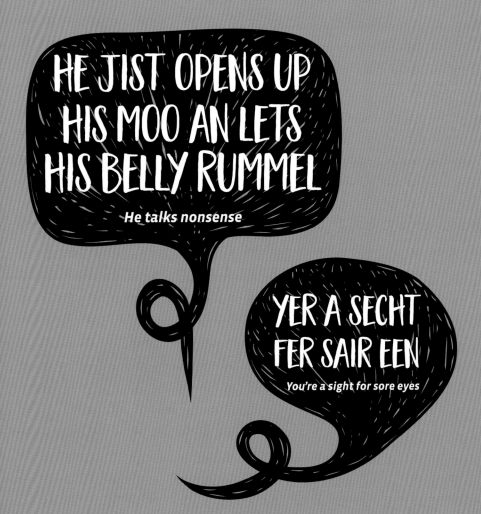

FACE
Physog

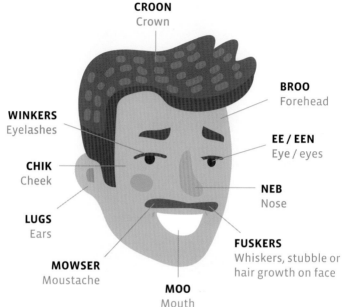

CROON
Crown

BROO
Forehead

WINKERS
Eyelashes

EE / EEN
Eye / eyes

CHIK
Cheek

NEB
Nose

LUGS
Ears

FUSKERS
Whiskers, stubble or
hair growth on face

MOWSER
Moustache

MOO
Mouth

AT INGINS ARE GAARIN MA EEN WAATER

Those onions are making my eyes water

GIE YER NEB A WEE DICHT WI A HUNKIE

Give your nose a wee wipe with a hanky

STOP LUGGIN IN!

Stop eavesdropping!

MA, AT LOON POKED ME RICHT IN THE EE!

Mum, that boy poked me right in the eye!

NEEN O' YER CHIK OR I'LL SKELP YER DOWP

None of your cheek or I will slap your bottom

ANATOMY
Pairts o' the body

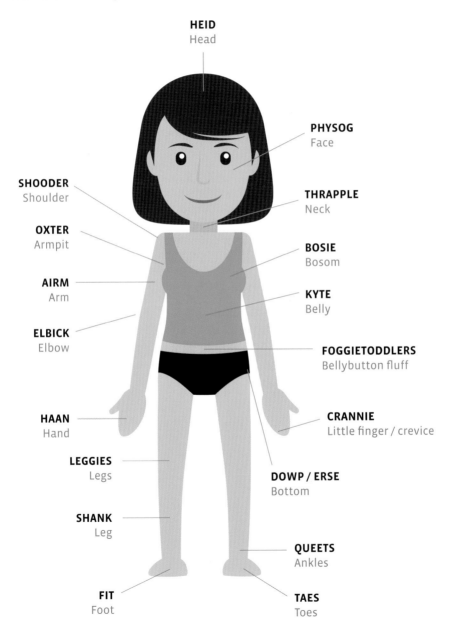

HEID
Head

PHYSOG
Face

SHOODER
Shoulder

THRAPPLE
Neck

OXTER
Armpit

BOSIE
Bosom

AIRM
Arm

KYTE
Belly

ELBICK
Elbow

FOGGIETODDLERS
Bellybutton fluff

HAAN
Hand

CRANNIE
Little finger / crevice

LEGGIES
Legs

DOWP / ERSE
Bottom

SHANK
Leg

QUEETS
Ankles

FIT
Foot

TAES
Toes

DIV YE KEN YER ERSE FAE YER ELBICK?
Do you know what you are doing?

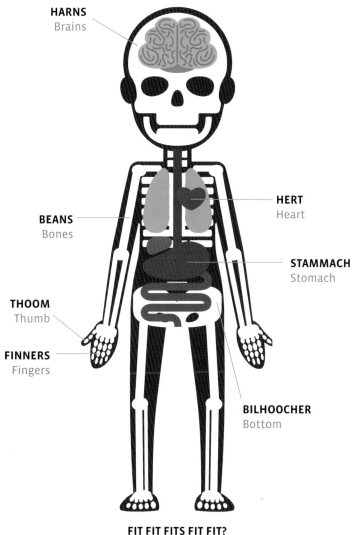

HARNS
Brains

HERT
Heart

BEANS
Bones

STAMMACH
Stomach

THOOM
Thumb

FINNERS
Fingers

BILHOOCHER
Bottom

FIT FIT FITS FIT FIT?
What foot fits what foot?

AT THE DOCTORS
Gingin te the doctors

FIT'S WRANG WI YE?
What is wrong with you?

FOO'S YER ERSE FUR PLEUKS?
Are you in good health?

FITS AILIN YE?
What is wrong with you?

FIT'S A DEE?
What is up?

FERFOCHAN
Exhausted

FOOSHIONLESS
Lacking energy

WABBIT
Weary

BOG O' SWYTE
Pouring with sweat

MA QUEETS HIV SWELT
My ankles have swollen

LOST MA VYCE
Lost my voice

NAE FEELIN WEEL AT AA
Felling very unwell

MA HEID'S LIKE A POT O' BROTH
I've got a headache

PLAISTER
Plaster

PEEL
Pill

POODER
Powder

CRAICHLY HOAST
Chesty cough

CANNA SEE
Poor vision

GAAN DEEF
Going Deaf

FAN'S SHE BETTER?
When is her due date?

WIPPIT
Wound

BYLE ON MA DOWP
Boil on my behind

BARKIT KNEE
Skinned knee

STOBBIT TAE
Stubbed toe

SMOR'N WI THE CAAL
Full of the cold

FEELING UNWELL
Nae weel

FALSERS
False teeth

SAIR FINNER
Sore finger

SAIR HEID
Sore head

YARKIT QUEET
Sprained ankle

PEELY-WALLY
Pale / sickly

MA HARNS HURTIN
My brain hurts

NEEDIN MAIR BUNDUGES
Need more bandages

JUNDIES
Jaundiced

SAIR BEANS
Sore bones

FEELIN HET
High temperature

PEEN IN MY BREIST
Heart attack

MA KYTE'S CHURNIN
Gastroenteritis

NAE KIPPIN
Insomnia

DUNT ON THE HEID
Bump on the head

LUBSTER REID
Sunburnt

KOWKIN
Feeling sick

BLEEDY COUTER
Nose bleed

BELLY-RIVE
Stomach-ache

TRAVEL

Seein the wurld

FAR ABOOTS ARE YE FAE?
Which part of the world are you from?

FURRY BOOTS ARE YE?
What is your current location?

GETTING THERE
Gettin aboot

DINNA LEAVE YER BUGGAGE UNATTENDID
Do not leave your bags unattended

PIT YER TRAY TABLIES AWA
Put your tables away for landing

FA ARE YE FLEEIN WI?
Which airline are you travelling with?

POOTLIN ABOOT
Going at a leisurely pace

HAE A WEE RUNNIE OOT
A drive in the countryside

ASKING DIRECTIONS
Speirin furry boots is...

FAR CAN YE CATCH THE BUSSIE TAE BUNCHORY?
Where can I find the Banchory bus stop?

FAN'S I NEXT BUS TAE UNION STREET?
When is the next bus for Union Street

DIV YE KEN FAR THE DUTHIE PARK IS?
Do you know where The Duthie Park is?

CAN YE PYNT ME IN THE DIRECTION O' BENACHIE?
Can you show me which way to go for Benachie?

IN FUT DIRECTION DIV I GING FOR BALMEDIE?
In which direction do I go for Balmedie Beach?

FAR ABOOT IS...
Where is...

FURRY BOOTS IS...
Where is...

I CANNA FYN IT
I can't find it

GING UP TE THE TAP O' THE BRAE
Go up to the top of the hill

TURN RICHT AAT THE TRAFFICLICHTS
Turn right at the traffic lights

CAIRRY ON
Carry on

AT THE HOTEL

YE'LL BE STAYIN ON THE TAP FLEER
You're in the penthouse

PLACES TO GO
Places te ging

MITHIR KIRK
St Nicholas Church

MITHIR TAP
View from Benachie

SHOPPIN CINTRES
Union Square / Trinity / Bon Accord / St Nicholas

BRIG O' BALGOWNIE
Bridge of Balgownie

PARK WI THE REID TRAINNIE
Seaton Park

PARK WI THE WINTER GAIRDENS
Duthie Park

PARK WI THE CRITTERS AND AAT FYTE SNAKE
Hazlehead Park

WORK

GYAD SAKES MIN
I'm not pleased

DINNA BE A SMART-ERSE
Don't be a know-it-all

YE'LL DEE AS YER TELT!
It's my way or the highway

PU UP YER BREEKS MIN
Put some effort into it

YIV NAE RUMGUMPTION
You've no good sense

YER EESLESS
You're useless

IF YE WINT A JOB DEEN AND DEEN WEEL, DEE IT YERSEL
If you want a job done, and done well, do it yourself

YER LIKE A DYEUK OOTA WAATER
You're out of your element

OCCUPATIONS
Jobbies

HEID BUMMER
The boss / manager

WORKS IN THE ILE
Oil worker

SCAFFIE
Street sweeper

JYINER
Joiner

PINTER
Painter

GAIRDENER
Gardener

FITBALLER
Footballer

INGINEER
Engineer

PRISINTER
Presenter

IN THE OFFICE
Deein wirk

**KEEP YER NEB TE
THE GRIN-STEEN**
Apply yourself
conscientiously
to your work

STICK IN NOO
Work hard

TIME TE GET YOKIT
Time to get started

**HE DISNAE LET THE GIRSE
GROW ANITH HIS FEET**
He doesn't ever stand still

HE'S A DAB HAAN AT AAT
He's good at that

HE'S A GRAN WIRKER
He works hard

I'M NAE SE GREEN AS I AM CUBBAGE LOOKIN
I'm not as daft as I look

MA HEID'S IN A JUMMLE
I'm jumbled-up

**DEEIN MA
DAILY DARG**
I'm doing my
daily work

**HING ON A MINTIE,
I'LL NEED TO REBEET**
Hold on while I restart
my computer

**DINNA FASH
YERSELF**
Don't trouble
yourself

**YIV GOTTEN
THINGS IN A
FANKLE**
You've got
things in a
muddle

**ROWE UP YER
SARK SLEEVES**
Get stuck in

**WID IT BE ONYWHERE
NEAR LOWSIN TIME?**
Is it home time yet?

**I JIST CANNA GET
MA HEID ROON IT**
I can't understand it

**IT TAAKS A WEE FYLIE TE GET
THE ILE OOT O' THE GRUN**
It takes a while to extract oil

IT'S A SAIR TRACHLE
Considerable effort

I WIRK AFFSHORE, TWA WIKS ON, TWA WIKS AFF
I work offshore on a bi-weekly rotation

TEAMWORK
Wirkin thegither

CAN YOOS NAE WIRK THEGITHER?
Can you try to work as a team

MONY HAANS MAAK LICHT WORK
Many hands make light work

TRY TE HAE JYNED-UP THINKIN
Produce an integrated
and coherent result

FIT A LOT O' HET AIR
Meaningless talk

**FIT'S YER RIZZONS FER
CHYNGING AAT?**
Can you explain why you've
made that revision?

AAT'S JIST A WEE BITTIE AFF I' WAA
That's quite an unconventional
approach you're taking

LET'S NAE FORGET THE MUCKLE PICTER
Let's not get bogged down in detail

PERFORMANCE REVIEW
Foo are ye deein?

DINNA GET YER DANDER UP!
Keep calm!

FAIR SCUNNERT
I'm fed up

FEEJEE
Angry

ARE YOU NAE WYSE?
I'm questioning your
professional judgement

ARE YOU FER REAL?
I'm questioning your
professional integrity

**I SMELL SHARN
FAE A BULL**
I detect bullsh*t

**AAT NEW LOON'S
A BIT O' A TOOTEROO**
The latest employee is
not very clever

HE'S A FEEL GYPE
He's a daft fool

**HE'LL NIVVER SET THE
HEDDER ON FIRE**
He's a bit dull

HE'S AA OWER THE PLACE
He's disorganised

HE'S AN AFFA SKIVER
He's work-shy

WHAT NEXT?
Fit neist?

Wint to ken mair?
If you would like to hear some Doric phrases being spoken, visit YouTube and search 'Doric for Beginners'.

Wint to share yer ain Doric word or phrase?
If you would like to share a Doric word or phrase, email doricforbeginners@gmail.com

Wint to buy this bookie, Doric gifts, cairds and airt?
If you would like to buy a copy of this book or some Doric gifts online visit the Etsy store and search for 'BrambleGraphics'.

I'm delighted

THANKS
Ta very muckle

Folks that hiv been a gweed help:
My creative twin Jeannie Price, my real twin Catriona,
my lovely, supportive mum and dad and my gweed-hertit
brother Gav.

Design and Art Direction:
Karen Barrett-Ayres at Bramble Graphics.

www.bramblegraphics.com

Picters by:
Karen Barrett-Ayres, Oleg Beresnev, Evgenii Naumov,
Dmitry Kalabin, Irina Vyatokha, Anton Deviatnikov,
Narakorn Chanchittakarn, ssstocker and Taszanatasha.